First Baptist Church of Fall River

First Baptist Church, Fall River, Mass.

1781-1881 - Centennial Anniversary, Feb. 15, 1881

First Baptist Church of Fall River

First Baptist Church, Fall River, Mass.
1781-1881 - Centennial Anniversary, Feb. 15, 1881

ISBN/EAN: 9783337302252

Printed in Europe, USA, Canada, Australia, Japan

Cover: Foto ©Lupo / pixelio.de

More available books at **www.hansebooks.com**

FIRST BAPTIST CHURCH,

1781   FALL RIVER, MASS.   1881

CENTENNIAL ANNIVERSARY,

FEB. 15, 1881.

" *We have heard with our ears, O God our fathers have told us what work thou didst in their days in the times of old.*"—Ps. 44 : 1.

MEMORIAL SERMON

BY THE PASTOR,

REV. A. K. P. SMALL, D. D.,

Sunday Morning, Feb. 13, 1881.

✣ SERMON. ✣

———␥———

EXODUS 12: 14—" *And this day shall be unto you for a memorial.*"

INTERESTING memorials have marked the prominent events of sacred history. At special points, along the great historic journey, eminent leaders erected a stone, a pillar, a monument; established a festival, a convocation,—memorials of the facts to be particularly remembered.

The memorial of this text was to commemorate Israel's starting toward their promised home. The sprinkled blood, the seven days' feast, was to mark a perpetual memorial, throughout all their generations, each year. But the memorial to which we now come has but one place, in the longer year of ten decades. Once approaching it, must be, to us, for the first and last time.

Ignoble would be forgetfulness of our Christian ancestry. Whatever of value belongs to this church, makes it the debt of gratitude to remember its birthday, which occurred a hundred years ago. That birthday scene—how impossible to have reproduced. An accurate photograph of that scene, would now be—

what a prize, what a remarkable relic.   To discern
faintest outline of it, we must peer through the mists
of imperfect record and tradition, to a point more than
seventy years beyond the limits of the present city
history, more than thirty years beyond the first Post
Office in this town, more than twenty years beyond the
time when the wild river of leaping falls gave name to
the town; when the quick-running, falling water,—
Quequechan,—was flowing free through its own wilderness career; more than thirty years before it was
first harnessed to machinery for changing cotton into
yarn, which must then be woven by hand in private
dwellings; and more than sixty years before intrusive
City Hall or Granite Block presumed to plant themselves over it, depriving the sparkling waters of their
natural right to the light of the sun.

This church, therefore, has been a factor of the entire history of this community, since its germ village, in
the outskirts of Freetown, was at Steep Brook, in the
darkest year of the revolutionary war, when, amid the
struggles of pioneer courage and peculiar faith, this
church had its birth, commencing the line of history, extending through the most eventful century,
the more interesting details of which it has been
assigned to others, most appropriately, to recount.

Since it is not expected of me to enter, now, into
particulars of this family history, which will be so
fully set before you, it may be only my part, at the
opening of these memorial services, to allude to the
opening of the history which is to be traced; to some
of the facts connected with the opening of this sacred
household.

The design of a memorial is to make real what
is to be remembered.   Were it possible for me to take

you back to the real scenes of that starting point, I
could ask for nothing more interesting than for you to
stand there, for these moments, and look around, catching as much as possible of the answer to this question :
What was the actual situation then? What some of
the main facts connected with the organization of this
church?

We now break completely loose from everything
modern, going back a century in a moment, to be with
the great-great-grandfathers and grandmothers of a hundred years ago. We go through the air; and turning
our great horoscopic telescope, to look through the
other end, we now see them there—the Boomers, the
Freemans, the Crockers,—the original thirty of this
church. Their antique little village, of a dozen dwellings and a hundred inhabitants, on the bank of the
river—how quiet, although in constant excitement.
They are thirty years distant from any clatter of a
cotton mill; and the infant just born, to live seventy
years, will die before the town will be disturbed by
sound of a locomotive engine.

The war claims first attention. The British from
Newport have recently been as near as Stone Bridge,
and all industry and economy cannot furnish requisite
supplies for home and for the army. Continental
money is becoming nearly worthless. Four months'
pay of a soldier will hardly procure a bushel of wheat,
and the pay of a colonel scarcely furnishes sufficient
oats for his horse. In some private houses is a small
forge, where the boys spend the evenings in making
nails. The pianofortes in constant use are the spinning
wheels and hand looms ; for the aristocracy of the
colony, including the governor and lieutenant governor,
have just entered into an agreement to wear only home-

spun clothes, and a spinning match is held at the house
of Rev. Mr. Murry, in Newbury, on which interesting
occasion he preaches a sermon from this text :

EXODUS 35 : 25—"*And all the women, that were wise
hearted, did spin with their hands.*"

Once a week the shrill horn of the mounted mail-
carrier is heard, when a copy of the little Boston
Gazette, of coarse brown paper, dropped at the grocery,
may give some tidings of General Washington's movements : and if a letter arrived from any great distance,
some whole family must combine to raise the two
shillings eight pence postage. On a Sunday morning, the people are coming, in their very best, from
Freetown, Dartmouth and Tiverton, the men with
continental three-cornered hats, plated buttons and
knee buckles, the good wife mounted on the pillion
behind her husband, and coming, not to a meeting-
house, but to the private residence of some brother,
where they are to enjoy a good feast of their own kind of
preaching from some visitor, perhaps Elder Thompson, of Swanzey.

At such a time, what brings them together for the
organization of a church ? It was not their pre-eminent wisdom, or knowledge of the greatness of the
work which they commenced. The peculiar greatness
of the New England fathers was, faithfulness in their
own places, as essential links in a chain of movements
greater than they ever projected, of the end of which
they had no conception, God working through them
vastly more than they knew.

Was it supreme wisdom of human statesmanship
for the Old Congress, in New York, six years after the
organization of this church, to pass an ordinance for
the government of a certain wilderness northwest of

the Ohio river, forever excluding slavery from it? When that wilderness territory had become the great Western States, with one-fourth of the population of the republic, Chief Justice Chase, referring to that famous ordinance of 1787, which had been called "the pillar of cloud and fire" for the imperial West, said it had "mightily exceeded" all thought or anticipation of those who passed it. Those organizing this church saw nothing of its future. It had in visible prospect, only such self-denying struggles against peculiar disadvantages as to offer nothing for worldly ambition. We must listen to their own words; and while looking, with our historic telephone catching now the actual religious conversation and preaching of that time, we find that those disciples were particularly influenced by their interest in fundamental gospel truth, particularly those doctrines of experimental religion which they found to be apostolic and in accordance with their own experience. Because of a remarkable history, their distinctive position was evidently taken with special reference to these three fundamental points: Personal regeneration; an apostolic church of regenerated members; and the church, with Christ alone as Head, entirely free from all political or State control. Not, as so many have supposed, was their special interest for the mere form of an ordinance, so much as for the privilege of any gospel ordinance distinct from State ordinances. Their special grief was an enforced connection with the State Church, which did not regard conversion essential to membership, or even to a place in the ministry.

After the great Whitefield awakening, more than twenty ministers of the State Church, or Standing Order, as it was called, at one time, in Massachusetts

alone, were brought to acknowledge that they had
never before known Christ. But the special church
action at that time was most particularly influenced
by the peculiar legislation concerning religion.

We alluded to a birth-day of peculiar courage. Did
it require special courage for a few peasant disciples
to unite for the quiet worship of a church? Ah! if it
was a Baptist church. Taking the position of a Baptist church, had cost banishment. During the hundred
previous years, back to the time that the first little
church had been driven farther into the Swanzey wilderness from Rehoboth, the position of a Baptist had
required more courage than that of a soldier in the
army. It had cost sharper persecution, hardship,
suffering, than British rulers ever attempted in this
country. Too incredible and distant that now seems
for any notice, only as a centennial mention of most
useless fossils, of which nobody cares to preserve a
specimen. It seems impossible that the most prominent thing before the minds of those organizing this
church was the fact that, for taking that position, some
of their friends had recently been fined; their cattle,
farming tools, household furniture, had been seized
and sold ; some persons had been publicly whipped,
imprisoned, or banished from the colony.

Why? The explanation is very easy. The State
Church was virtually the political power, or a prominent element of it. Entrance to it was made easy
without a gospel profession of faith, for those wishing
to belong to the dominant power, for the support of
which all citizens must be taxed. Then, of course,
Baptists must be silenced, or banished, since they
stood for the idea that worship should be free ; that
the Gospel Church is a volunteer spiritual body, entirely

free from State control; that it is not the province of civil law to control spiritual life. To silence that idea, how many since the days of the apostles " have had their utterances hushed in martyrdom!"

The relation of the ecclesiastical to the civil power has been a problem of the ages. That is really the perplexing problem in many countries in the Old World to-day. Even enlightened Christian England does not yet clearly see through it. The difficulties of that problem sent both Puritans and Pilgrims to American shores. But how imperfect the solution, even in their own minds. Religious liberty was the ostensible object of their search. But how long and tenaciously they clung to the idea that it must be the liberty of State authority to control the worship of every man, or banish him from citizenship. Though acknowledging Jesus as King, how slow to understand His own declaration, that His kingdom is not of this world; its conquests not by the force of civil power.

In that world-wide struggle for separation of Church and State, for liberty to worship in simple apostolic order, it has seemed to be the special call of Baptists, in this and other countries, to stand for centuries almost alone; to stand, Sir Isaac Newton said, " the only body of Christians that had never symbolized with the Church of Rome;" in whose code of laws, established in Rhode Island, said Chief Justice Story, " we read for the first time since Christianity ascended the throne of the Cæsars, the declaration that conscience should be free." That declaration had cost double banishment; first from the Old World to the wilds of this coast, then from the jurisdiction of Massachusetts Bay to the wilderness retreat which, in grati-

tude for his almost miraculous escape, Roger Williams
called Providence, almost two hundred years before
that declaration found complete legal sanction in this
Bay State.

According to the record of Mr. Backus, " the Baptists were driven into the wilderness, were scourged by
order of the civil power, were spoiled of their goods,
were cast into prison, were pelted by violence of mobs,
were falsely accused; their principles were caricatured,
their petitions slighted."

After many years of vain attempts to obtain from
the General Court their share of the common rights,
which the Charter of William and Mary guaranteed
to all, ten years before the organization of this church,
the Warren Association resolved to send to the British
Court for defence of liberty, which the more oppressive
colonial enactments denied to them ; yet the Baptists
were so hearty in the desire for national liberty that
" they were exceedingly reluctant to lay their com-
plaints at the foot of the throne." At length came on
the great Revolution, and that was for what ? What
moved all the people to such union in that heroic
struggle ? The hope of freedom from oppression.
What oppression ? Britain had, indeed, put a tax
upon tea. Nobody was compelled to buy it. A petty
tax upon tea, or commercial paper, had caused no
suffering, no confiscation of goods, or imprisonment.
But the unjust principle of the smallest taxation without representation, aroused united patriotism to resist
it. Yet, strange to say, in the very year before the
opening battle of Lexington, eighteen members of a
Baptist church were imprisoned in Northampton jail,
for refusing to pay taxes to a church in which they had
no representation. The odious tea they could toss into

Boston harbor, but they were obliged to swallow the preaching of the government minister, though both taste and price were more unwelcome.

Like the loyal slaves in our late war, they confidently hoped the struggle of the Revolution would bring a recognition of their citizen and Christian rights. But in the very midst of that war, within the year of the organization of this church, Massachusetts adopted its new State constitution, in which, despite most earnest discussions, remonstrances, entreaties, were retained elements of the same oppressive enactments; the puritanic statesmen still thinking it would be unsafe for the State to allow entire freedom of worship. John Adams then said, "A change in the solar system might be expected as soon as a change in that ecclesiastical system of Massachusetts." The position of a Baptist church could not, then, have been chosen for popular favor: it was, indeed, almost outside the limits of any fellowship.

For mutual encouragement, four widely separated churches had united to form the Warren Association, fourteen years prior to this organization. But sad experience had made Baptists so fearful of religious combinations, that for eighteen years this church ventured no connection, even with that Association of its own faith, preferring to stand in independent loyalty to Christ as only Master and Lord.

Hence the courage referred to, of that birth-day,—venturing to take that name and place at just the time when, as a recent historian records it, the newly adopted constitution "made every Baptist church in Massachusetts an outlaw, to be uprooted and destroyed, or only suffered to exist under restrictions."

Thus have we stood with those pioneers, looking

around upon the precise condition of things, on the
fifteenth day of February, 1781, in the fifth dark year
of the Revolutionary war, when this church was
organized.

The honored and deeply lamented historian of
Brown University, in an able review five years ago,
alluded to the "contemptuous treatment" which the
Baptist petitioners for liberty received from the Massachusetts delegation to the Continental Congress, and
said :—"It is only when we recall such facts, that we
can appreciate the full extent of the Revolution in
public sentiment which the past century has witnessed."

And now, from the stand-point of that birth-day
of 1781, how shall we safely return to our home of
1881 without trespass upon the intervening century
history, through which others are to be competent
guides, this afternoon ? We must come as we went,
through the air; while, for safe guidance, our flight
over the hundred years may be just near enough to
earth for glimpses at the line of those on the watch
towers.

Our point of departure is at a private house, where
the original thirty become "The Baptist Church of
Christ in Freetown, Dartmouth and Tiverton." Two
years down the sacred line, in another private house,
we discern Rev. Amos Burrows receiving ordination
to be pastor for one year. Twelve years farther on,
at another ordination scene, appears that remarkable
watchman, "blind as to natural sight, but having such
spiritual light as to be esteemed a clear preacher of
the gospel," who, with fourteen years of colleague
assistance, at different times, by pastors Boomer, Ross
and Miner, continued to be the chief shepherd of the
flock for thirty-eight years, when, like rejoicing Simeon,

Father Borden might well have felt ready to depart, so nearly reaching the memorable event of 1833,—this long sought amendment to the State Bill of Rights: "All religious sects and denominations, demeaning themselves peaceably and as good citizens of the Commonwealth, shall be equally under the protection of the law; and no subordination of any one sect or denomination to another shall be established by law."

To secure this, the Baptists took their stand in Rhode Island a hundred and ninety-seven years before, the religious victory which, at the birth of this church, seemed to him who was to be the second President of the Republic as little to be expected as a change in the solar system. God moves not as the wisest man foresees! But onward we fly over the fourteen years, during which the honored Bronson is the pulpit waymark, as pastor, then son-in-law, in the flourishing family of the eldest daughter; then—O, can we not pause in our flight, to live again through the next eight years with those whom we had hoped to see standing together here to-day, that the whole family might rise up again in the honored presence of pastors Hotchkiss and Mason.

Onward, through the next seventeen years, we seem to be catching the benediction of those now receiving higher honors than any church on earth can give,—pastors whose names need not here be spoken,—too early in heaven, it seemed to us. We are passing almost within the tones of pastor Eddy's voice, after which the church has reached such strength and amazing magnanimity as almost to surpass the patience of the persecuted fathers in enduring in the pulpit, the smallest of all; and now, so quickly again on this side the century history, in our present position, we may perhaps stand for another moment, and look around upon what would have been a hundred times more wonderful to our ancestors of a hundred years ago. Their best glasses caught no glimmer of our times.

Where are the conflicts of that birth-day? That proved to be almost the crisis day of both the national and ecclesiastical struggles. Those peculiar battles were then nearly over, and, "like a receding thunder-storm, their noise has long since died away on the far horizon." Fortunately, this church had its home in this place, where public sentiment never sanctioned religious persecution. On this point of territory, between the river and the sea, the atmosphere was always too free for the intermeddling of official troubles.

Churches of other denominations, thirty-five years later, began to assist in forming a neighborhood of Christian families, whose whole career has been one of remarkable harmony and fraternal co-operation. Rev. Mr. Fowler left this record:—"Though this people are divided into so many sects, each of which is neither slow nor timid to assert and defend its distinctive doctrinal peculiarities, yet perhaps there is no town in New England where more general harmony prevails, or kinder neighborhood intercourse is enjoyed, or where the members of different denominations shake hands more cordially."

The amazing progress of the century can be claimed by no single church, denomination or department of life, while the changes may be nowhere more remarkable than in the particular to which our present survey must be confined. This church, instead of remaining alone, looking out upon one little Baptist Association in all New England, is now connected with fourteen Massachusetts Associations, of two hundred and eighty-nine churches and nearly fifty thousand members. It lives to see the churches of its denomination in the whole country increase from 500 to 26,000, and their membership from 55,000 to 2,296,327.

It was thirty years after the organization of this church, when our first missionaries left for foreign lands; now we have almost a thousand churches and more than eighty-five thousand members in Europe and Asia, the largest missionary membership of any denomination in America : only three of our benevolent societies—the Missionary Union, the Home Mission, and Publication Society—expending three-fourths of a million dollars annually. Instead of one little college, its building occupied for military barracks, its president an army -recruiting officer, as a hundred years ago, its present honored head—worthy successor of Manning and Wayland—with us to-day, may now consider himself father of more than thirty vigorous Baptist colleges, eight theological seminaries, some fifty academies, in which may now be ten thousand students, in this country, with many more abroad, indicating our item toward the advancing light and cultured manhood of the world. The reported increase of our churches for the last ten years is at the rate of fourteen each week, or two each day. While the whole population of the country, including the immense immigration, chiefly of other sects, has been increasing only twenty-four per cent., the Baptist increase has been fifty-one per cent.

As due expression of gratitude, how appropriate to stop and turn from everything else, once in a century, for united thanksgiving for such a remarkable history of blessing and enlargement. This, certainly, has not come from any pre-eminent excellence of our people; not because they have greatly surpassed others in purity, learning, wisdom or holiness. It would be safer and more modest to accept, as the secret of such peculiar growth, the explanation of that eminent authority of another denomination, already quoted. This is the statement of Prof. Diman :—" The Baptists made their appeal to Scripture, as the sole authority. To that fundamental principle, through all their history, they have steadfastly adhered. The famous maxim, " The Bible—the Bible only," has found with them its most consistent advocates ; and their growth was, in a large part, a democratic protest against exclusiveness—a stand for equal religious rights."

How singular a prevalent idea, that the chief Baptist peculiarity is exclusiveness, so exactly contrary to the fact that their distinctive position was chiefly a protest against the exclusiveness of any superior culture, or power, or sect,—a position for largest liberty, for equal religious privileges. And such growth, according to this historic authority, seems to have been because their distinctive position proved to be for those principles which God, for the honor of His own Word, and the common people, for their own liberty, must have vindicated. And how wonderfully they have been vindicated. This church has lived to see all the people now perfectly united in the enjoyment of equal religious liberty : rejoicing in not now claiming to be distinguished from other denominations in requiring a confession of personal faith, as a condition of church membership.

" Those principles," says a recent writer, " are now the accepted faith of Christendom." And, evidently without thinking how delightfully he was turning that old solar system illustration, this writer adds:—" Those principles for which the fathers so long contended and suffered, would no more be questioned to-day than the movements of the earth around the sun, or the force of gravitation,"—his way of saying "Solar System."

The Baptists can, by no means, now claim peculiarity in the idea that those coming to the Communion should be the baptized church. And whatever seems to remain of their special distinction now, with what remarkable unanimity the highest Biblical authorities declare it is eminently Scriptural: impressing this lesson, that the hope of the church is not in improved human devices, or the secured comforts of a few, but clinging to the simplicity of the Word and Christ-like zeal for elevating and saving all the people. Our fathers proved that, even in weakness, armed with eternal truth. they could triumph through adversity. It remains to see if the sons, careless of the truth, will make shipwreck of prosperity.

The church of a hundred years ago! Where is that? How long since all its members. and their children, passed from earth. How soon not one of all these thronging congregations of to-day will be among the living. At the next anniversary, not one of our children, or children's children. may be the living historian, to recount the events through which we are now passing. But the church is not dead; it lives, and will live. Its foundation remains unshaken. Its future has the security of covenant divine. This branch of the church lives, not houseless, as a hundred years ago, but in its honored sanctuary, from which, one year ago to-day. was the triumphant removing of all incumbrance; and with its parsonage—perhaps too beautiful and comfortable—what furnishing and vantage ground, if now thoroughly reconsecrated to Christ, for a new century career.

Therefore, it is peculiar honor and gratification for me to be permitted to echo the hearty welcome to the gathering, with the fathers, mothers, brothers, sisters, friends, around the sacred hearthstone, for these successive services. In renewing of spiritual life and covenant, for united onward career, under the special divine benediction, may it prove to be a blessed Memorial unto you.

INTRODUCTORY NOTE.

It is due to Brethren DAWLEY and BLAISDELL to have it distinctly stated, that the following are not the interesting historical addresses, as delivered by them on the anniversary occasion. The Committee, as instructed, omitting portions important for public address, took large liberty in arranging the interesting matter furnished in the addresses, with added details, in the direct order of events, for convenience of reference, thus sacrificing rhetorical beauty for a connected record of plain historic facts.

HISTORY of the CHURCH,

BY HON. J. E. DAWLEY.

The earliest extant record of the church, the centennial anniversary of which we now celebrate, is found in exactly this form :

"Febuary the 15th day 1781.
then was Established the 2nd baptis church of Christ In Freetown, In fellowship with Elder Thompson's and Elder Luises Churches."

It is supposed that the organization of the church was in the house of one Jonathan Brownell, that stood on what is now North Main street, east from the house of worship of the Third Baptist Church. There were thirty constituent members of the church,—sixteen men and fourteen women,—whose names may be found in a church manual. On the 22d of May, 1783, was the ordination of the first pastor—Elder Amos Bur-

rows. The ordination service was conducted by Elders
Thompson of Swanzey, Burrows of Tiverton, and Goff
of Dighton, in the house of Samuel Warren. After an
unfortunate pastorate of one year, Mr. Burrows removed to Vermont. It seems that a regular church
meeting was held on the second seventh day in each
month, that "George Crocker was appointed to keep
the church book," and that those meetings were considered as important as preaching services, since it was
"Voted, that our stated meetings should not be set
aside, notwithstanding a minister should be present at
any such meeting."

Five years after Mr. Burrows left, the church chose
two of their own useful and promising young men,
"To improve their gifts in public, and to attend meetings where they shall be requested;" and three years
later, appears an arrangement for more regular public
worship. It was voted that one of those brethren,
who from his eighteenth year had been blind, "should
improve one half of the Lord's day, that Brother
Nathaniel Boomer read the psalm, and that Mathew
Boomer take the lead of the singing." After three
years more proof of their real worth, on the third
Thursday of May, 1795, occurred the double ordination of those two young men, James Boomer and Job
Borden. The ministers participating in the ordination
service were Elders Thompson, Burrows,* Hathaway
and Baker. During the same month the church invited
Joseph Stillwell and Nathaniel Boomer "to act as
deacons till some should be chosen." Four years later,
in 1799, the church joined the Warren Association.

For about eight years the two pastors labored
faithfully together, when a threatening cloud is indi-
cated by this record of Dec. 9, 1803 :—"This day is a

trying scene to us; both our Elders think of leaving us;—may the God of Heaven protect us." And God did protect them, for while Elder Boomer asked for his dismission to go to Charlton, where he died Feb. 24, 1837. Elder Job Borden remained the honored pastor of the church.

On June 13, 1789, was a meeting of a committee "concerning the Meeting House." That first Meeting House, at the Narrows, must have been opened for worship about the year 1800, when the church, which for some time had been known as "The Church in Freetown, Dartmouth and Tiverton," by a second change of name, came to be called "The Second Baptist Church in Tiverton."

"The church *in Tiverton*, under the pastoral care of Elders James Boomer and Job Borden," invited a council to meet at the house of Gamaliel Warren, Oct. 30, 1799, when there was the triple ordination of James Reed as an itinerant preacher, and Nathaniel Boomer and Joseph Stillwell as deacons. Two years later— Nov. 13, 1802—is found in the records this first allusion to the new meeting house:—"Chose George Crocker to have the care of the meeting house." Plainly, then, worship commenced in that house between 1799 and 1802.

There are but brief records of the church for the next twenty-five years; this single item giving a glimpse of the public worship:—"Sept. 2, 1813, chose John Davol to read the *him, &c.,* in publick."

During the two years 1827—1829, Rev. Arthur Ross acted as colleague pastor, receiving a part of his support for services as school teacher. Those two years are memorable for the first great revival in the history of the church, in which more than ninety were added

to its membership; for the third change of the name
of the church, when it became "The First Baptist
Church of Troy; for the building of the second meeting house; and the organization of "The Baptist
Female Charitable Society," one of whose first enter-
prises was "to procure the trimmings and dress the
meeting house."

Mr. Ross was born in Thompson, Conn., in 1791;
ordained in 1819. A great revival attended his first
pastorate. After six years in Connecticut and two in
Fall River, he was pastor in Bristol. Coventry, War-
wick, Newport, Lonsdale, Natick, and, finally, in
Pawtucket, where, in Christian triumph. he died June
16, 1864. His talents, studiousness and piety made
him a man of remarkable power. He published several valuable historical pamphlets, and during his
ministry baptized more than fourteen hundred persons.

The new meeting house referred to was the one on
South Main street, afterwards sold to the Episcopal
church. It was dedicated July 30, 1828. The sermon
was preached by Elder Choules of Newport; and on
the evening of the same day, Enoch French and John
Davol were ordained as much needed younger deacons;
and at the next meeting it was voted " that the church
be considered a Sunday School Society."

In connection with the new village meeting house,
appeared an evident tendency toward fashion. It was
voted to purchase candlesticks for the evening meetings, the Association was invited, and N. White, R.
Wrightington and William Ashley were appointed to
" seat the house;" and Deacon French, A. Hall and
P. Smith were chosen to take charge of the bass viol.
It is possible that the violins were in such demand
elsewhere that three church officers could not exercise

exclusive control of them. Fortunately, perhaps, there followed some checks to undue vanity, for it was voted "to withdraw fellowship from Israel C. Durfee for his remarks respecting building our meeting house, in which he manifested a covetous disposition, and for his *unrichous* remark in relation to our young deacons, French and Davol."

Elder Seth Ewer was obtained to supply the pulpit for the year 1829.

The interesting young preacher, Rev. Bradly Miner, was next called to the pulpit. He was born in North Stonington, Ct., July 18, 1808 ; was converted and baptized in his thirteenth year; and having studied at Newton, Mass, and Hamilton, N. Y., was ordained at Fall River, July 14, 1830. Elders Ewer, Perry, Phillips, Choules, Welch, Philleo, with Elders Webb, of the Methodist, and Smith, of the Congregational church, participated in the interesting ordination services. He successfully filled the office of pastor for about three years, when, being still a young man, he felt constrained to resign for the opportunity of more study and renewed health. He was afterward settled in Pawtuxet and Woonsocket, R. I., at Dorchester and Pittsfield, Mass., and lastly with the Friendship Street Baptist Church in Providence, where, amid abounding labors and signal ministerial prosperity, he suddenly died Oct. 28, 1854. He was remarkable for a soft, musical voice, animated manner, fervent piety, rare industry and wisdom, and during his ministry he baptized about four hundred persons.

About the time that Mr. Miner left, the venerable senior pastor passed from earth. That remarkable man, blind from his youth, but of rare attainments, of sound common sense, the large hearted, devoted, faith-

3

ful minister, universally honored, after more than forty
years of labor with the church of his youth, died Dec.
31, 1832, aged 77 years. The church entered upon its
record a grateful tribute to his memory, a full account
of the largely attended funeral, (when the sermon was
preached by Elder Welch of Warren,) and of the long
procession of citizens following his remains to the
place where they rest, beside those of his wives, in the
old graveyard at the Narrows, near where the first
house of worship stood. On his tombstone is found
this inscription :—" He was an exemplary Christian,
a sound divine, an acceptable preacher, a judicious
counselor; in short, a good minister of Jesus Christ."
" Howl, fir tree, for the cedar is fallen."—*Zach.* 11: 2.

The church, a little past its half century point, had
then reached a peculiar period of transition from the
older to the later generation. Attention was soon
turned to the one who was to be the leader into a new
career of growth and prosperity. Rev. Asa Bronson
became pastor April 4, 1833. He was a man of peculiar power and efficiency, remarkable for strength,
soundness, richness of gospel resources and a warm
heart, rather than for polished rhetoric. During the
previous year, the Church and Society had been divided
into twenty districts, each assigned to particular persons for religious visitation ; and three years later,
sixteen brethren were appointed as special overseers of
as many divisions of the church. About that time
revised articles of faith were adopted, and Abiathar
Hall and Stephen L. French were elected deacons. In
1835 the modest little MEH-SHWAY-EE SOCIETY appeared, like an obscure fountain, whose broadening
stream of pure, life-giving waters has steadily been
flowing on for forty-five years.

In 1834, the name of the town was changed from Troy to Fall River, when there must be the fourth change in the name of the church : and in 1836, the " Female Charitable Society of Troy" adopted a new constitution, by which the name became " The Fall River Baptist Female Benevolent Society." In the same year, the church became one of the constituent members of the Taunton Baptist Association.

The first covenant meeting was held in the vestry of the new house of worship, called the Temple, July 1, 1840, and that house was dedicated Sept. 16 of that year. Some years before, the church had recorded this resolution : " That we most earnestly and affectionately invite all the members of the church who are not not now members of the Temperance Society, immediately to become members, and throw all their influence in favor of Christian sobriety." Then followed the great Anti-Slavery struggle, in which this church took a foremost and unequivocal position. During the earnest discussions of the decade, from 1840 to 1850, the bold pastor, deacons and members introduced, defended and had recorded, as the adopted sentiments of the church, such declarations as these : " Slavery is one of the aggrossest sins ainst God and violations of the rights of man that can be committed." " No circumstances justify holding slaves." " This church, as an independent body, feels bound to bear its unequivocal testimony against the abominable sin of slavery." " We will not invite, or *allow*, a slaveholding minister to occupy the pulpit, or invite or allow a slaveholder to commune with us as a church." In June, 1850, it was voted that the third Thursday evening in each month be observed for religious conference and prayer on the subject of slavery : and in

the letter to the Association, in September of that
year was an expression of the views of the church
against the sin of slavery.

The church was blessed with two remarkable re-
vivals, and during the eleven years of Mr. Bronson's
pastorate seven hundred and nine were added to the
church.   He was afterward pastor at Albany for two
years, when he returned and became pastor of the
Second Baptist Church in this city, and died Nov. 29,
1866, aged 68 years.   He was succeeded in this church
by Rev. V. R. Hotchkiss, who was publicly recognized
as pastor Dec. 4, 1845, the sermon on that occasion
being preached by Rev. William Hague of Boston.
With rapidly increasing population, the Baptist portion of the field had become too large for a single
church.   In all the Sunday Schools under its supervision, eleven hundred members were reported.   The
time had come for new arrangements.   The Second
Baptist Church was recognized in September, 1846,
to become members of which about a hundred and
seventy persons were dismissed from the First Church,
which, by the fifth change of name, then came to be
the " First Baptist Church of Fall River."   The preaching of Pastor Hotchkiss was clear and logical, peculiarly rich in exposition, giving instruction to the
church and sowing seed for the future.   Leaving this
church in 1849, he was pastor of the Washington
Street Church in Buffalo, N. Y., for about six years,
when he accepted a Professorship in Rochester Theological Seminary.   Having honorably filled that position
for ten years, he was drawn back to his former position in Buffalo, where, for another period of fourteen
years, he was the able pastor and preacher, and of late
has been giving to the students of several Theological

Institutions rich fruits of his thought and experience in lectures upon Expository Preaching.

The house called the "Temple" was conveyed to the Second Church in October, 1847, from which time this church worshipped in "Union Hall" till the first Sunday in 1850, when Rev. A. P. Mason having become pastor, the church entered the vestry of the new house on North Main street, which completed house was dedicated Oct. 23d. On the evening of the same day was the ordination of Rev. A. W. Carr, who was then a member of this church. Rev. R. E. Pattison, D. D., was one of the preachers, and the veteran missionary, Rev. J. M. Haswell, brother-in-law of Pastor Mason, was one of the large number of ministers united in the services of that very interesting day.

Mr. Mason was a lineal descendant of the Samson Mason who was an officer in Cromwell's army. He came to America in 1650, and settled in Dorchester; then removed to Rehoboth, and afterward, "for conscience sake," to Swansea, where he assisted to build the Baptist meeting house, for which he was summoned before the authorities of Plymouth Colony, fined fifteen shillings, and warned to leave the jurisdiction of the Colony. From that true Baptist stock descended our Pastor Mason, during whose faithful ministry of three years was an interesting revival, in which fifty-nine valuable members were added to the church. He was afterward pastor in Chelsea, and for several years has been District Secretary of the American Baptist Home Missionary Society.

The next beloved pastor—Rev. Jacob R. Scott—could be retained here for only the year 1853. He was educated at Brown University and at Newton. He was pastor at Petersburg and Hampton, Va., Portland,

Me., Fall River, Mass., Rochester and Yonkers, N. Y., and finally Superintendent of Schools in Malden, where he died Dec. 10, 1861, aged 46 years.

After his resignation, Rev. Jonathan Aldrich successfully supplied the pulpit for nearly a year of delightful revival work, when Daniel J. Glazier was elected pastor. He was a young man of great promise, a graduate of Brown University and beloved by all who knew him. He was "the Student Preacher" of the beautiful biography written by his pastor, Dr. Turnbull. Before taking the place, for which he seemed so peculiarly fitted, he suddenly died March 9, 1855. It was a great disappointment and affliction to the church. But one soon came to the vacant place, whose name will long continue to awaken most tender memories. Rev. P. B. Haughwout became pastor in 1855. His rare and varied qualities, it is impossible to describe. He was scholar, naturalist and preacher. It was difficult to tell in which department he was most brilliant. He had been called "the eloquent boy preacher," and was ordained when twenty-one years of age. He was pastor, for brief periods, of four churches, in Michigan and New York, before coming to Fall River. His enthusiasm for books, for science, for the pulpit, was always beyond the endurance of his physical strength. In 1860 he went to Europe, remaining seven months, during which time the church ordained, and had for acceptable supply, Rev. A. Judson Padelford, and was blessed with an interesting revival. Pastor Haughwout gave to this church fifteen years of his most vigorous life, during which was his enthusiastic share in the great struggle against rebellion, and the addition of more than two hundred to the church, when failing health made retirement essential. Afterward he supplied the church in Dunkirk two years; then became pastor of the church in Jamestown, N. Y., where he very suddenly died April 26, 1877, in the 49th year of his age.

In 1871. Daniel C. Eddy, D. D., became pastor. The house of worship was extensively remodeled and enlarged. The former pastors, Drs. Hotchkiss and Mason, with other clergymen of the city, took part in the interesting re-dedication services Sept. 3, 1872. On the evening of the first Sunday in the re-dedicated house, eleven persons were baptized. At nearly the same time, those members who had been connected with the Mission at Bowenville were organized into the Third Baptist Church. After a rich revival, in which more than sixty were added to the church, Dr. Eddy closed a two years' pastorate, and was succeeded by the present pastor in 1874. During the next year the parsonage, which was purchased in 1868, was removed, and a new, beautiful parsonage was built.

During the year 1879 the city was blessed with a very remarkable and extensive revival, in connection with the preaching of Rev. Mr. Pentecost, the evangelist, as a result of which about seventy were added to this church. After a season of unusual business depression and financial disasters, Sunday, Feb. 8, 1880, was a day of very remarkable interest, when the Church and Society, with wonderful unanimity, courage and benevolence, rose up and cancelled the Society debt of $20,000, and they come to this great anniversary with their excellent buildings paid for.

The names of pastors are mentioned, because they may be more prominent waymarks on the watch towers, not because they are more deserving than other pillars of the church. The first two deacons, Stillwell and

Boomer, served the church, the one thirty-seven, the
other forty-seven years.   Their mantles fell on worthy
successors—Deacons Enoch French and John Davol—
both men of remarkable piety, Christian experience
and devotions to the interests of the church, wonderfully adapted to the duties of their time and place, and,
in the family line of each, is a successor in the deacon-
ship, worthily maintaining the honor of their sacred
memory.   Deacons Philip Smith, John E. Carr and
Benjamin Buffinton. a trio of congenial spirits, followed
in that honorable line.   They were earnest, consistent
men, adorning their profession, honoring their office,
serving God and the church.   Their memory is blessed.

Those with, O what a company of the fathers and
mothers, are among the departed; but whom fond
memory has, almost visibly, among these gathering
memorial guests.

Love hallows every spot we tread.
    And memory is sweet beside,
And, close, the living and the dead
    Walk, loving, side by side.
They come to cheer: and, oh, how much
    We need them here, our love to share !
They come to bless, we feel their touch,
    It thrills. and everywhere
The mortal and immortal meet :
    Time sinks into a shoreless sea ;
And now, thank God, their loosened feet
    Tread on eternity.

Following the departed deacons, are Abiathar Hall,
Stephen L. French and Seth Pooler, of the veterans,
still remaining, with those younger deacons, who, by a
later arrangement, have been elected for briefer terms

of services,—Jesse F. Eddy, Joseph L. Buffington, Edward Warren, Henry Richards, Geo. S. Davol and Henry S. Buffinton. With these might be mentioned the names of many valuable members, still living. But the time for their eulogy is not yet,—may it long be delayed.

With the most prominent and useful men, might, as properly, be mentioned the line of noble women who, since the organization of the "Woman's Charitable Society" in 1828, for more than fifty years have continued the benevolent work for the poor and needy, gladdening many desolate hearts and homes, "the work still going on, the only changes being that the names of those who rest from their labors are replaced by the children and grand-children of those whose lives are precious legacies to the church." None would regard it invidious to mention the single name, so beautifully connected with the origin of that little "Meh-Shway-ee Society,"—the eminent example of Christian greatness in little things, author of "*Beginning to do Good*" and "*Continuing to do Good*,"— Laura H. Lovell, of blessed memory.

> " Sister, a little time, and we
>   Who knew thee well, and loved thee here,
>   One after one shall follow thee
>   As pilgrims through the gate of fear,
>   Which enters on eternity.
> Yet shall we cherish not the less
>   All that is left our hearts meanwhile ;
> The memory of thy loveliness
>   Shall round our weary pathway smile.
> Like moonlight when the sun has set—
> *A sweet and tender radiance yet.*"

Beside the ordinations already mentioned, the church ordained William Knapp, and it has licensed to preach Lorenzo Lovell, James Smithies, Andrew D. Milne, Alexander Carr and Charles E. Smith, all of whom became useful pastors except James Smithies, who died immediately after he became a licentiate.

The Missionary Concert is observed on the first and the Sunday School Concert on the second Sunday evening in each month, and there are regular Sunday collections for benevolent purposes. The Sunday School and mission work will be duly recorded elsewhere.

Such is but a meagre outline of the history of the church for a hundred years ; and this is probably the brighter portion of it. We are not to suppose that all were days of sunshine in the time of the fathers. Each step of their progress was through trials. It is noticed that the member whose name stands first on the record was almost immediately a subject of discipline. He was judged unworthy to have charge of the church book ; but it is an encouraging example of faithful discipline to find that about twenty years afterward he was found in the faithful care of the meeting house.

The total membership of the church, for the century, has been not far from 1700, the larger part of whom are beyond the river of death. How soon shall we be of that number. But may the ever-living Head of the Church continue to raise up, for its membership, those who shall be as good pastors, deacons,—men and women as faithful of good works in the coming as in the past century.

Oh Father, from Thy throne on high
Look down upon us all the while,
And cheer us with thy loving smile,
As on the circling years gone by.

Uphold us when with weariness
  We fall or falter by the way,
  And may Thy presence, every day,
Our pathway cheer, our duties bless.

On heavenly manna may we feed,
  And waters of salvation drink ;
  Give comfort more than we can think,
And send us only what we need.

Our pleasures temper, dry our tears,
  Drive from our hearts all fear of ill,
  With love our cup of blessing fill,
And guide us through the rolling years.

Beneath the shelter of this home
  The shadow of Thy presence cast ;
  As Thou hast blest us in the past,
Bless us a hundred years to come.

HISTORY of the SUNDAY SCHOOL.

BY HON. J. C. BLAISDELL.

As early, perhaps, as 1815, a Miss Tilson, afterward Mrs. Job Borden, who kept a public school in the second building from the corner of Borden street, on South Main, invited her scholars, who had wandered about on the Sabbath, to come to her school rooms on the Sabbath for Bible instruction, and then to go with her to church.   There is no record of any organization, but acting independently, with true Christian zeal, there were thus planted, by her personal efforts, seeds which blossomed into glorious fruitage.

Early in the spring of 1827—a year memorable for an interesting revival, and for the building of the first meeting house, on South Main street,—a Sunday School connected with the Baptist church was organized; its constitution providing "that the school shall commence at 8 o'clock and close at 10 1-2 in the morning; that it shall be enjoined upon the scholars to attend public worship; that any male member who neglects to attend shall be subject to a fine of six cents, unless excused by the President; and that none but persons of steady and moral habits shall be admitted members of the Society." The constitution provided for the election of proper officers, who, by a sub-committee of three, were to take charge of the school, which was to hold its sessions from April to October.

This school was held in a building called "The Cradle of Liberty," on the corner of Pleasant and Second streets. Under this constitution, the school continued its work till 1829, when a new constitution was adopted making the school an auxiliary to the "Rhode Island Sabbath School Convention." In 1836 it withdrew from the Rhode Island Convention and united with the Massachusetts Union. At the same time, Jonathan Brayton was elected the first Superintendent, the school having previously been conducted by the committee of the board of officers. They also established branch schools, one at the Globe, one on the back road, one called the North School, and one at Steep Brook; these all under the care of superintendents and assistants sent from the home school. All the schools were closed during the winter, and reopened in the spring.

In 1837 additional branch schools were established; one called the Gardner School, and one at Bowenville, for the support of which the late M. H. Ruggles annually contributed five dollars, and one over the ponds. In December the superintendents of the various branch schools made their reports to the Board of Managers of the home school. It was in this year that delegates were first sent to the Teachers' Convention connected with the Taunton Baptist Association. Stimulated by the glowing results of previous work, by the widening field and great increase of Christian workers, in the spring of 1840 the Board entered with renewed zeal upon the work of sustaining the various branch schools. With the superintendents, they sent out committees to reach all the people of every grade, bringing them under religious influence, till the village was environed with Sunday Schools. The various superintendents were instructed to bring the bills of their expense to the treasurer. It was made the duty of a special committee to find among the members of the church such persons as seemed most suitable for superintendents and teachers, making such changes as seemed essential; and so successful was the earnest, united work, that at the annual meeting in March, 1841, it was reported that more than eleven hundred teachers and scholars were connected with the various schools under the supervision of the Society; and after more than forty years, at Steep Brook, at the Globe, at New Boston, over the ponds, and elsewhere, are clearly visible the fruits of those Sunday School Missions in the regular worship of organized churches. In 1846 the time had come, with increasing population of a prospective city, for new organizations. The Second Church was established, and to it was given the care of such branch schools as then existed.

In 1847, the pastor, Dr. Hotchkiss, was requested " to visit every member of the church and congregation, and procure a pledge from them that they will attend the Sunday School, or give sufficient reason for not doing so."

In 1859, a Mission School was established in the basement of a building at the corner of Spring and Mulberry streets, and it now holds its sessions in a building erected for it by the First Baptist Society, it being now known as the " Columbia Street Mission School," and is the only mission school now under the care of the church. In 1868, a Mission School was established by the Board at Bowenville, which resulted in the organization of the Third Baptist Church in 1871. In 1873, by a change in the constitution, the school came under the government of the church. The infant department has been an important and peculiarly interesting branch of the school, the superintendents of which have rendered themselves worthy of special mention. The first of these, Miss L. H. Lovell, is remembered with special interest. Two years before she became Superintendent of the Infant Sunday School, in her own secular school she organized the little Meh-Sway-ee Society, which for forty-five years has kept a gospel light shining in heathen lands. Following her, as faithful and successful superintendents of that department, have been Mr. T. A. Francis, Miss A. C. G. Canedy, Mr. Joseph L. Buffington and Miss Ellen M. Shove.

Another important branch of the school has been the large Bible Class. It was first called the "Bethany Bible Class," under the instruction of Bro. Jesse F. Eddy, afterwards taught by Bro. J. E. Dawley, and for several years has been under the direction of Bro. J. C. Blaisdell.

The honored Superintendents of the whole school, retained in their places by successive annual elections, and released when removal from the city, or other providential events have rendered it necessary for them to resign, have been :

Jonathan Brayton,........................1836—1839
John Eddy,.............................1839—1843
George G. Lyon,.........................1843—1846
John Eddy,.............................1846—1847
Joseph E. Dawley,.......................1847—1849
Henry Richards,.........................1849—1856
J. C. Blaisdell,. ....1856—1873

George S. Davol,........................1873—1874
Spencer Borden,........................1874—1876
Jesse F. Eddy,.........................1877—1878
Walter J. Paine,.......................1879—1880
Joseph L. Buffington,...................1880

With these faithful and successful men, are held in grateful remembrance the noble company of their co-workers, assistant superintendents, teachers, members of various boards and committees,—such indispensable helpers, who have shared so largely in this good work, which still goes on with such increasing promise as should enlist the hearty co-operation of all true disciples, since its importance is greater than can be measured by years or centuries.

APPENDIX.

Centennial Anniversary.

A committee on Decorations was appointed, consisting of the following persons :—Mr. and Mrs. Geo. W. Dean, Mr. and Mrs. Geo. B. Durfee, Mr. and Mrs. Edward A. French, Mr. and Mrs. Enoch J. French, Mrs. J. F. Eddy, Misses Dora Durfee, Mary Tripp, May Lindsey, Emma Davol, Messrs. William Lindsey, Jr., Jesse E. Blaisdell and J. Clarence Read. They earnestly entered upon their work, and, with the assistance of many willing helpers, most satisfactorily completed it. Heavy festoons, vases of beautiful exotics, bouquets, wreaths, mottoes, and the portraits of pastors and deacons, arranged most tastefully, gave to the church a charm, of which an artist caught a beautiful picture.

The organist—Mr. Bennett—and Mr. V. W. Haughwout were a committee on music. They arranged to have the various services interspersed with the more celebrated ancient church music, which contributed very peculiar interest to the occasion.

Sunday Morning.

Memorial Sermon by the pastor. Text, Ex. 12 : 14, " *And this day shall be unto you for a memorial.*"

Sunday Afternoon.

Historical Addresses by Hon. J. E. Dawley and Hon. J. C. Blaisdell.

Sunday Evening.

Sermon by Rev. E. G. Robinson, D. D., President of Brown University. Text, 1 Cor., 10 : 21, " *Whatsoever ye do, do all to the glory of God.*"

By masterly argument, historical facts and forcible illustrations, it was clearly shown that, for many best reasons, it is the highest, the only true life, to do all things for the glory of God.

Tuesday, Feb. 15.

This was strictly the anniversary day. A reunion of the older present and past members of the Society was held in the parlors of the meeting house in the afternoon, at four o'clock. Dea. Henry S. Buffinton, of the Committee of Arrangements, spent much time in securing the attendance of the venerable members. He gathered these facts of that occasion :

"More than two hundred attended, three-fourths of whom were upwards of sixty years of age. Among the company were forty persons whose ages averaged seventy-five years. There were present thirty-eight past members, who were dismissed to organize the Second Church, thirty-five years ago. The oldest person present was Phebe Prince, a colored sister, who was formerly a slave in New York, and who is now about ninety years of age. Three deacons of the church were present, who had obtained a ripe old age :—

Abiathar Hall, eighty-three; Seth Pooler, seventy-eight; and Stephen L. French, seventy-seven years old. Having spent two hours in delightful social intercourse, the venerable company sat down to tea, at the head of the table being eight persons who united with the church more than fifty years ago."

It was a remarkable occasion, when many of those fathers and mothers were together for the last time. After tea, a few of the more infirm were conveyed to their homes; the others joining the larger audience up stairs for

The Evening Service.

The choir sang "Strike the Cymbal." Rev. James Boomer offered prayer. Brief addresses were made by Dr. Mason, Rev. Mr. Padelford, Rev. E. M. Hunt of the Second, and Mr. Dyer of the Third Church, Dr. Adams and Rev. Mr. Burnham of the Congregational Churches. Letters were read from former pastors and friends, and also these lines, written several years ago by the late Pastor Haughwout:

Why should we fret, and fume, and worry,
    And rack our bones on sleepless couches,
And steam through life with rush and hurry,
    Only to die with well-filled pouches?
A pluck or two,—the world is bare!
    And if we lived in pain or laughter—
Or lived at all—in fact, who'll care
    A thousand years or so hereafter?

Like caterpillars, from our vitals
    We spin the web that we delight in,
To find, at last, our sole requitals
    A shroud to wrap our souls from sight in;

And life is short—we soon spin out,—
   And if we spin with tears or laughter,
'Twill be the same—what man can doubt ?
   A thousand years or so hereafter.

We laugh to-day, and weep to-morrow,
   And smiles and tears are cheaply bought ;
We laugh because we know no sorrow,
   And weep to find we've laughed for naught.
But life is short, and death will scatter
   Our sighs, and smiles, and tears, and laughter ;
And when we're through, what will it matter
   A thousand years or so hereafter?

There's but one thing worth holding fast,
   When all is said, and all is done—
The hope that when this world is passed
   A better world will be begun ;
Though life is short, and death will scatter
   Our sighs, and smiles, and tears, and laughter,
That's something that will greatly matter
   A thousand years or so hereafter.

Finally, a poem was read, and touching allusions were made to departed friends, by Mr. A. K. Slade.

The company then returned to the vestry rooms for refreshments and social reunion, and thus closed Memorial Services of very peculiar and indescribable interest.

www.ingramcontent.com/pod-product-compliance
Lightning Source LLC
Chambersburg PA
CBHW021442090426
42739CB00009B/1601